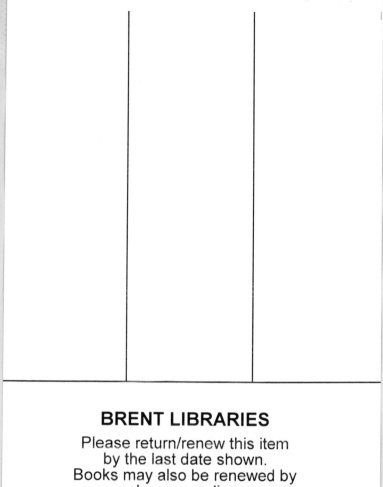

BRENT LIBRARIES

Please return/renew this item
by the last date shown.
Books may also be renewed by
phone or online.
Tel: 0333 370 4700
On-line www.brent.gov.uk/libraryservice

FACT CAT

ROSA PARKS

Izzi Howell

WAYLAND
www.waylandbooks.co.uk

FACT CAT

Get your paws on this fantastic new mega-series from Wayland!

Join our Fact Cat on a journey of fun learning about every subject under the sun!

First published in Great Britain in 2016 by Wayland
Copyright © Wayland 2016

All rights reserved
ISBN: 978 0 7502 9771 4
Dewey Number: 323.1'196'073092-dc23
10 9 8 7 6 5 4 3 2 1

MIX
Paper from responsible sources
FSC® C104740

Wayland
An imprint of Hachette Children's Group
Part of Hodder & Stoughton
Carmelite House
50 Victoria Embankment
London EC4Y 0DZ

An Hachette UK Company
www.hachette.co.uk
www.hachettechildrens.co.uk

A catalogue for this title is available from the British Library
Printed and bound in China

Produced for Wayland by
White-Thomson Publishing Ltd
www.wtpub.co.uk

Editor: Izzi Howell
Design: Rocket Design (East Anglia) Ltd
Fact Cat illustrations: Shutterstock/Julien Trone
Front cover illustration by Wesley Lowe
Consultant: Kate Ruttle

Picture and illustration credits:
Alamy: Everett Collection Historical 4, The Protected Art Archive 9, Everett Collection Historical 10, Everett Collection Historical 11, World History Archive 12t, World History Archive 13, Pictorial Press Ltd 18; Corbis: Bettmann 15, Bettmann 16, Paul Sancya/Pool/epa 20; Getty: Don Cravens 7, Grey Villet 14; Library of Congress: Leffler, Warren K 5, Leffler, Warren K 8, Trikosko, Marion S 17; Shutterstock: Joseph Sohm title page, Everett Historical 6, Joseph Sohm 12b, Joseph Sohm 19; US Government: Architect of the Capitol 21.

Every effort has been made to clear copyright. Should there be any inadvertent omission, please apply to the publisher for rectification.

The author, Izzi Howell, is a writer and editor specialising in children's educational publishing.

The consultant, Kate Ruttle, is a literacy expert and SENCO, and teaches in Suffolk.

FACT CAT FACT

There is a question for you to answer on most spreads in this book. You can check your answers on page 24.

CONTENTS

Who was Rosa Parks? 4

Early Life 6

A Segregated World 8

Group Meetings 10

The Bus Protest 12

The Montgomery Bus Boycott ... 14

After the Boycott 16

The Civil Rights Movement 18

Later Years 20

Quiz 22

Glossary 23

Index 24

Answers 24

WHO WAS ROSA PARKS?

Rosa Parks was an **activist** in the 1950s. She grew up in the **USA** at a time when there was a lot of **racism**. Black and white people didn't have the same **rights**.

Rosa Parks **protested** against the way that black people were treated on buses. They were not allowed to sit at the front.

When other people saw Rosa Parks standing up for the rights of black people, they decided to join in. This was the beginning of the **civil rights movement** in America.

Civil rights activists took part in **peaceful** protests, such as **marches**.

FACT CAT FACT

Civil rights activists often held peaceful sit-ins at restaurants. They would sit in one area and refuse to leave.

EARLY LIFE

Rosa Parks was born in 1913 in the south of the USA. As a child she lived with her mother, her brother and her grandparents.

Rosa went to a school for black children, similar to this one. She had to leave school when she was 16 to look after her sick grandmother.

FACT CAT FACT

Rosa's mother was a teacher. She taught Rosa that getting an education was very important. What was the name of Rosa's mother?

When Rosa Parks was 19, she decided to go back to school and finish her exams. After that, she worked in a shop as a **seamstress**.

Sewing clothes was hard work. Rosa sewed many items of clothing every day.

A SEGREGATED WORLD

In the early 20th **century**, many southern American **states** had **laws** that **segregated** black and white people. Black people couldn't go to the same places, such as restaurants and public toilets, as white people.

This taxi company only served white customers.

Across America, some white people made black people's lives difficult. It was hard for black people to vote or buy a house. In some places, black people couldn't get married to white people.

At schools that weren't segregated, some white students would treat black students badly.

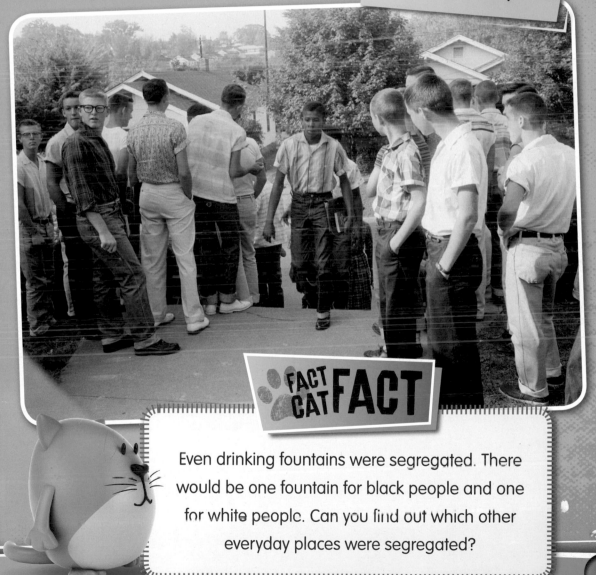

FACT CAT FACT

Even drinking fountains were segregated. There would be one fountain for black people and one for white people. Can you find out which other everyday places were segregated?

GROUP MEETINGS

Rosa Parks was part of the NAACP – a group that fought for the rights of black people. They wanted the government to make sure that everyone was treated the same.

The NAACP found new members by calling people on the phone and telling them about the group.

Some white people were angry that this group was asking for equal rights. They threatened some members of the group. Some members were even attacked and killed.

Going to NAACP meetings was dangerous. Rosa Parks kept going because she knew it was important to fight for her rights.

N.A.A.C.P. MEETING

FACT CAT FACT

You can still be a member of the NAACP today. What does NAACP stand for?

THE BUS PROTEST

On 1 December 1955, Rosa Parks got on the bus to go home from work. In Montgomery, the city where she lived, black people could only sit at the back of the bus.

On 1 December, the black section of the bus was full so Parks sat at the front, in the white section.

The bus that Rosa Parks protested on is now in a museum.

PLEASE HAVE EXACT FARE READY

2857

When a white man got on to the bus, the driver asked the black people in the white section to stand up so that the white man could sit down. Rosa Parks didn't move. She thought that black people should be able to sit anywhere on the bus.

When Parks refused to give the white man her seat, she was arrested and taken to the police station. In this photo, the police are taking her fingerprints.

FACT CAT FACT

Rosa Parks had to pay a $10 **fine** for breaking the law. What other punishments do people get for breaking the law?

THE MONTGOMERY BUS BOYCOTT

After Rosa Parks' arrest, some people organised a bus **boycott** to show that they were unhappy. Black people in Montgomery wouldn't travel by bus until they could sit anywhere on the bus.

FACT CAT FACT

Organisers printed 35,000 leaflets to let other people know about the boycott. On which date did the Montgomery Bus Boycott begin?

Most black people walked to work during the Montgomery Bus Boycott.

Rosa Parks was happy that her actions **inspired** other people to protest. However, she had some bad experiences because of the boycott. She lost her job and her family was **threatened**.

Martin Luther King Jr organised the Montgomery Bus Boycott. He was a good **public speaker**, and encouraged people to take part.

AFTER THE BOYCOTT

Nearly a year later, in November 1956, the American **courts** decided that it was **illegal** to segregate buses. Black people could finally sit wherever they liked, just like white people.

Martin Luther King Jr celebrated the end of the Montgomery Bus Boycott by sitting next to his white friend on the bus.

FACT CAT FACT

The Montgomery Bus Boycott ended on 20 December 1956. How many days did it last?

Some white people were angry that the buses in Montgomery weren't segregated any more. They shot at the buses with guns.

Some white people were so angry they **bombed** the houses of the boycott organisers.

DANGER
KEEP
OUT

THE CIVIL RIGHTS MOVEMENT

The end of bus segregation was just the beginning of the American civil rights movement. Martin Luther King Jr organised many more protests. His speeches inspired people to support equal rights.

In 1963, over 200,000 people came to Washington DC to listen to Martin Luther King Jr. What was the name of this famous speech?

In 1964, the American government passed a law that made it illegal to treat someone badly because of their **race**. It became easier for black people to vote and buy houses.

There are still problems with racism in the USA today. People still go on marches to show that they are unhappy.

50 YEARS LATER...
STILL MARCHING FOR FREEDOM JUSTICE VOTING RIGHTS
THE STRUGGLE CONTINUES

50 YEARS LATER...
STILL MARCHING FOR FREEDOM JUSTICE VOTING RIGHTS
THE STRUGGLE CONTINUES

FACT CAT FACT

In 2009, the USA elected its first black **president** – Barack Obama.

LATER YEARS

After the Montgomery Bus Boycott ended, Rosa Parks decided to move to a new city. She wanted to protect her family from people who didn't agree with the civil rights movement.

In 1999, the American government gave Rosa Parks a Congressional Gold Medal to celebrate her work in the civil rights movement.

FACT CAT FACT

The Congressional Gold Medal is one of the most important medals that a person can receive in America. Can you find out the name of another person who has been given one?

Rosa Parks died on 24 October 2005. When Parks was alive, she said, 'I would like to be remembered as a person who wanted to be free ... so other people would be also free'.

Thousands of people – black and white – came to see Rosa Parks' **coffin**.

QUIZ Try to answer the questions below. Look back through the book to help you. Check your answers on page 24.

1 When was Rosa Parks born?

a) 1913 ✓

b) 1930

c) 1955

2 Rosa Parks worked as a teacher. True or not true?

a) true

b) not true ✓

3 In the early 20th century, some restaurants and cinemas were segregated. True or not true?

a) true ✓

b) not true

4 What happened when Rosa Parks wouldn't give up her seat for a white man?

a) She was allowed to carry on sitting in the white section of the bus.

b) She moved to the black section of the bus.

c) She was arrested by the police. ✓

5 Black people stopped using public buses in the Montgomery Bus Boycott. True or not true?

a) true ✓

b) not true

GLOSSARY

activist someone who tries to change society

arrest to be taken by the police and asked questions about a crime

bomb to attack something or someone with a bomb that will explode

boycott when people stop using, buying or doing something that they don't agree with

century a period of 100 years. The 20th century refers to dates between 1900 and 1999.

civil rights movement a series of protests and marches in America in the 1950s and 1960s. As a result, a law was created making it illegal for black people not to be given the same rights as white people.

coffin the box that a dead body is buried in

courts a place where a judge decides if someone has committed a crime

fine money that you have to pay because you have committed a crime

illegal describes something that you are not allowed to do because of a law

inspire to make someone feel like they want to do something

laws the rules of a country

march an organised walk by a group to show that they don't agree with something

peaceful describes a way of doing something without violence

president the person in charge of the government

protest to show that you disagree with something

public speaker someone who gives speeches to a group of people

race a group of people that have the same skin colour and body type

racism when someone is treated badly or differently because of their race

rights the things that you can do or have, according to the laws of your country

seamstress a woman who sews clothes as a job

segregate to separate people from different races

state a part of the USA

threaten to tell someone that you will kill or hurt them

USA the United States of America

INDEX

arrest 13
attacks 11, 17

buses 4, 12–13, 14, 15, 16, 17, 18, 20

childhood 6–7
civil rights movement 5, 18–19, 20
coffin 21

government 10, 19, 20

marches 5, 19
Martin Luther King Jr 15, 16, 18
medals 20
Montgomery Bus Boycott 14–15, 16, 17, 20

NAACP 10–11

protests 4, 5, 12–13, 15, 18

racism 4, 11, 17, 19
rights 4, 5, 10, 11, 18, 19, 20

schools 6, 9
segregation 8–9, 16, 17, 18
sit-ins 5
speeches 18

ANSWERS

Pages 6–20

page 6: Leona McCauley

page 9: Some places include swimming pools, waiting rooms and shops.

page 11: National Association for the Advancement of Colored People.

page 13: Some punishments include going to jail or helping in the community.

page 14: 5 December 1955

page 16: 381 days

page 18: The 'I Have A Dream' speech

page 20: Some people include Martin Luther King Jr and Neil Armstrong.

Quiz answers

1 a - 1913
2 not true – she was a seamstress.
3 true
4 c - she was arrested by the police.
5 true

OTHER TITLES IN THE FACT CAT SERIES...

Space
The Earth 978 0 7502 8220 8
The Moon 978 0 7502 8221 5
The Planets 978 0 7502 8222 2
The Sun 978 0 7502 8223 9

United Kingdom
England 978 0 7502 8927 6
Northern Ireland 978 0 7502 8942 9
Scotland 978 0 7502 8928 3
Wales 978 0 7502 8943 6

Countries
Brazil 978 0 7502 8213 0
France 978 0 7502 8212 3
Ghana 978 0 7502 8215 4
Italy 978 0 7502 8214 7

History
Neil Armstrong 978 0 7502 9040 1
Amelia Earhart 978 0 7502 9034 0
Christopher Columbus 978 0 7502 9031 9
The Wright Brothers 978 0 7502 9037 1

Habitats
Ocean 978 0 7502 8218 5
Rainforest 978 0 7502 8219 2
Seashore 978 0 7502 8216 1
Woodland 978 0 7502 8217 8

Geography
Continents 978 0 7502 9025 8
The Equator 978 0 7502 9019 7
The Poles 978 0 7502 9022 7
Seas and Oceans 978 0 7502 9028 9

Early Britons
Anglo-Saxons 978 0 7502 9579 6
Roman Britain 978 0 7502 9582 6
Stone Age to Iron Age 978 0 7502 9580 2
Vikings 978 0 7502 9581 9

Animals
Mammals 978 0 7502 9598 7
Reptiles 978 0 7502 9602 1
Amphibians 978 0 7502 9599 4
Birds 978 0 7502 9601 4
Fish 978 0 7502 9600 7

WAYLAND
www.waylandbooks.co.uk